KU-626-568

hank you...

...for purchasing this copy of Spelling for Literacy for ages 7-8. We hope that you will find these 126 worksheets helpful as part of your programme of literacy activities.

Please note that photocopies can only be made for use by the purchasing institution; supplying copies to other schools, institutions or individuals breaches the copyright licence. Thank you for your help in this.

This Spelling for Literacy book is part of our growing range of educational titles. Most of our books are individual workbooks but, due to popular demand, we are now introducing a greater number of photocopiable titles especially for teachers. You may like to look out for:

HOMEWORK TODAY for ages 9-10
ISBN 1897737 24 6

HOMEWORK TODAY for ages 10-11
ISBN 1897737 48 3

NUMERACY TODAY for ages 5-7
ISBN 1897737 53 X

NUMERACY TODAY for ages 7-9
ISBN 1897737 63 7

NUMERACY TODAY for ages 9-11
ISBN 1897737 58 0

SPELLING FOR LITERACY for ages 5-7
ISBN 1897737 44 0

SPELLING FOR LITERACY for ages 8-9
ISBN 1897737 54 8

SPELLING FOR LITERACY for ages 9-10
ISBN 1897737 59 9

SPELLING FOR LITERACY for ages 10-11
ISBN 1897737 64 5

BEST HANDWRITING for ages 7-11
ISBN 1 897737 98 X

To find details of our other publications, please visit our website: **www.andrewbrodie.co.uk**

Andrew Brodie Publications

Suggestions for using this book...

We have examined carefully the current national policies for teaching spelling as part of your literacy work. In writing this book we have included all the spelling patterns and objectives which are specified within these policies. We have arranged the words into sets, usually of sixteen words. Each set of words is used in three styles of sheet:

Sheet A

✓ Can be photocopied onto OHP transparencies for discussion.

✓ Can be displayed on the wall as 'Words of the Week'.

✓ Can be copied onto card and cut up to make matching cards.

Sheet B

✓ Activity sheets to be used in the Literacy Hour.

✓ Can be hole-punched to go in pupils' personal spelling files.

✓ Can be given as homework sheets.

✓ **Answers provided on the last three pages of this book.**

Sheet C

✓ Has a fold line so that children can copy the words, then cover them to write again without looking.

✓ A perfect follow-up activity for the learning which has taken place using sheets A and B.

✓ Following the Learn, Write, Check system.

© Andrew Brodie Publications ✓ PO Box 23, Wellington, Somerset, TA21 8YX ✓ www.andrewbrodie.co.uk

Spelling for Literacy *for ages 7-8*

Contents

© Andrew Brodie Publications ✓ PO Box 23, Wellington, Somerset, TA21 8YX ✓ www.andrewbrodie.co.uk

Set 17 Sheets A, B & C	**Year 3, Term 2** Changing words by adding y	mess, messy, ink, inky, full, fully, fuss, fussy, mood, moody, sleep, sleepy, dream, dreamy, cheek, cheeky
Set 18 Sheets A, B & C	**Year 3, Term 2** Adding y to words with short vowels	fun, funny, run, runny, sun, sunny, tin, tinny, pop, poppy, dot, dotty, rat, ratty, bat, batty
Set 19 Sheets A, B & C	**Year 3, Term 2** Adding y to words ending in e	laze, lazy, ease, easy, smoke, smoky, shine, shiny, rose, rosy, stone, stony, breeze, breezy, bone, bony
Set 20 Sheets A, B & C	**Year 3, Term 2** Adding s to make plurals	boy, boys, girl, girls, table, tables, book, books, desk, desks, time, times, window, windows, house, houses
Set 21 Sheets A, B & C	**Year 3, Term 2** Adding es to make plurals	catch, catches, match, matches, push, pushes, brush, brushes, blush, blushes, fox, foxes, box, boxes, church, churches
Set 22 Sheets A, B & C	**Year 3, Term 2** Making plurals for words with a vowel then y	day, days, key, keys, tray, trays, monkey, monkeys, play, plays, holiday, holidays, birthday, birthdays, buy, buys
Set 23 Sheets A, B & C	**Year 3, Term 2** Making plurals for words with a consonant then y	baby, babies, lady, ladies, puppy, puppies, pony, ponies, party, parties, penny, pennies, hobby, hobbies, fly, flies
Set 24 Sheets A, B & C	**Year 3, Term 2** Strange plurals	man, men, woman, women, child, children, tooth, teeth, mouse, mice, goose, geese, calf, calves, wolf, wolves
Set 25 Sheets A, B & C	**Year 3, Term 2** Silent letters	knee, kneel, knife, knives, know, knock, gnat, gnome, write, wrist, wrap, wrapping, when, where, honest, rhyme
Set 26 Sheets A, B & C	**Year 3, Term 2** More silent letters	comb, bomb, thumb, crumb, lamb, numb, calf, calves, half, halves, calm, palm, could, should, would
Set 27 Sheets A, B & C	**Year 3, Term 2** Compound words	play, playground, motor, motorway, bed, bedroom, every, everybody, everyone, everything, some, somebody, someone, something, somewhere, sometimes
Set 28 Sheets A, B & C	**Year 3, Term 2** More compound words	pan, pancake, week, weekend, goal, goalkeeper, break, breakfast, stairs, upstairs, downstairs, any, anybody, anyone, anything, anywhere
Set 29 Sheets A, B & C	**Year 3, Term 2** Suffixes: ly	love, lovely, nice, nicely, like, likely, safe, safely, real, really, usual, usually, regular, regularly, proper, properly
Set 30 Sheets A, B & C	**Year 3, Term 2** Suffixes: ful	hope, hopeful, care, careful, pain, painful, use, useful, wonder, wonderful, cheer, cheerful, beauty, beautiful, till, until
Set 31 Sheets A, B & C	**Year 3, Term 2** Suffixes: less	hope, hopeless, care, careless, pain, painless, use, useless, home, homeless, speech, speechless, end, endless, harm, harmless
Set 32 Sheets A, B & C	**Year 3, Term 2** Suffixes: er	teach, teacher, farm, farmer, drive, driver, mine, miner, babysit, babysitter, run, runner, shop, shopper, spin, spinner
Set 33 Sheets A, B & C	**Year 3, Term 2** Using apostrophes	is not, isn't, was not, wasn't, did not, didn't, does not, doesn't, will not, won't, cannot, can't, could not, couldn't, should not, shouldn't

© Andrew Brodie Publications ✔ PO Box 23, Wellington, Somerset, TA21 8YX ✔ www.andrewbrodie.co.uk

Set 34 Sheets A, B & C	**Year 3, Term 2** More apostrophes	I would, I'd, I have, I've, they have, they've, she will, she'll, there is, there's, where is, where's, here is, here's, they are, they're
Set 35 Sheets A, B & C	**Year 3, Term 3** Prefixes: mis, non, im, ex, in, co, anti	behave, misbehave, sense, nonsense, fiction, non-fiction, stop, non-stop, import, export, interior, exterior, star, co-star, clockwise, anti-clockwise
Set 36 Sheets A, B & C	**Year 3, Term 3** Prefixes: bi, re, tri, dis, in, ab, pre, inter, sub	cycle, bicycle, recycle, tricycle, appear, disappear, visible, invisible, normal, abnormal, view, preview, review, interview, marine, submarine
Set 37 Sheets A, B & C	**Year 3, Term 3** Days	Monday, Tuesday, Wednesday, Thursday, Friday, Saturday, Sunday, holiday, yesterday, tomorrow, birthday, anniversary, weekday, weekend, fortnight, tonight
Set 38 Sheets A, B & C	**Year 3, Term 3** Months and seasons	January, February, March, April, May, June, July, August, September, October, November, December, spring, summer, autumn, winter
Set 39 Sheets A, B & C	**Year 3, Term 3** Numbers	eleven, twelve, thirteen, fourteen, fifteen, sixteen, seventeen, eighteen, nineteen, twenty, thirty, forty, fifty, sixty, seventy, eighty
Set 40 Sheets A, B & C	**Year 3, Term 3** Numbers and measurements	ninety, hundred, thousand, million, metre, centimetre, millimetre, kilometre, gram, kilogram, litre, millilitre, second, minute, hour, month

Within the National Literacy Strategy, the spelling objectives are heavily weighted towards Term 2, which is quite often the shortest term.

You may wish to work on some of the Term 2 spellings towards the end of Term 1 and at the early part of Term 3.

The three Contents sheets can be photocopied and used as individual or class records, by highlighting words as they are covered or learnt by the children.

© Andrew Brodie Publications ✓ PO Box 23, Wellington, Somerset, TA21 8YX ✓ www.andrewbrodie.co.uk

YEAR
3
Term
1

SET
1
Sheet
A

sing	singing
ring	ringing
walk	walking
jump	jumping
paint	painting
dress	dressing
rest	resting
call	calling

© Andrew Brodie Publications ✓ PO Box 23, Wellington, Somerset, TA21 8YX ✓ www.andrewbrodie.co.uk

Adding ing to the end of words (1).

These words have two consonants at the end.

We don't change them when adding **ing**.

Add **ing** to the words on the left.
The first one is done for you.

sing		singing
ring	**Two consonants**	
walk		
jump	**jump**	
paint	⬇	
dress	**jumping**	
rest		
call		

Fill in the missing words using some of the **ing** words that you have made.

When I am _____ I put on my socks first.

When we went for a walk, Gina kept _____ up to touch the leaves.

I could hear Tom _____ my name.

I was _____ a picture.

The bells were _____ and I was _____ a song.

Now make up some sentences of your own, using words from the list above.

© Andrew Brodie Publications ✓ PO Box 23, Wellington, Somerset, TA21 8YX ✓ www.andrewbrodie.co.uk

YEAR
3
Term
1

SET
1
Sheet
C

1. Look carefully at each word.

2. Say the word out loud.

fold line

3. Copy each word in your best handwriting.

4. Look again at the first word, then fold the paper over it to cover it.

5. Write the word in COLUMN 3.

6. Check your spelling.

7. Now do the same for each word.

Learn, Write, Check.

Name:

Date:

LEARN THE WORD	WRITE THEN COVER	WRITE THEN CHECK
sing		
singing		
ring		
ringing		
walk		
walking		
jump		
jumping		
paint		
painting		
dress		
dressing		
rest		
resting		
call		
calling		

© Andrew Brodie Publications ✓ PO Box 23, Wellington, Somerset, TA21 8YX ✓ www.andrewbrodie.co.uk

YEAR **3** Term **1**

SET **2** Sheet **A**

sleep	sleeping
dream	dreaming
feel	feeling
shout	shouting
sail	sailing
boil	boiling
peel	peeling
speak	speaking

© Andrew Brodie Publications ✓ PO Box 23, Wellington, Somerset, TA21 8YX ✓ www.andrewbrodie.co.uk

These words have two vowels before the final consonant.

We don't change them when we add **ing**.

Add **ing** to the words on the left. The first one is done for you.

sleep

dream

feel

shout

sail

boil

peel

speak

Two vowels

slèep

sleeping

	sleeping

Fill in the missing words. The first one has been done for you.
Try to find an extra pair of words for each set.

sleep	→	sleeping	sail	→	
sweep	→		nail	→	
	→			→	

eat	→		look	→	
treat	→		cook	→	
	→			→	

Choose four of the **ing** words on this page. Write a sentence for each of these words.

© Andrew Brodie Publications ✓ PO Box 23, Wellington, Somerset, TA21 8YX ✓ www.andrewbrodie.co.uk

Learn, Write, Check.

fold line

1. Look carefully at each word.

2. Say the word out loud.

3. Copy each word in your best handwriting.

4. Look again at the first word, then fold the paper over it to cover it.

5. Write the word in COLUMN 3.

6. Check your spelling.

7. Now do the same for each word.

Name:

Date:

LEARN THE WORD	WRITE THEN COVER	WRITE THEN CHECK
sleep		
sleeping		
dream		
dreaming		
feel		
feeling		
shout		
shouting		
sail		
sailing		
boil		
boiling		
peel		
peeling		
speak		
speaking		

© Andrew Brodie Publications ✓ PO Box 23, Wellington, Somerset, TA21 8YX ✓ www.andrewbrodie.co.uk

YEAR 3 Term 1

SET 3 Sheet A

run	running
hop	hopping
sit	sitting
skip	skipping
step	stepping
grip	gripping
shut	shutting
win	winning

© Andrew Brodie Publications ✓ PO Box 23, Wellington, Somerset, TA21 8YX ✓ www.andrewbrodie.co.uk

Doubling the consonant to add ing.

Each of these words ends with a consonant with one vowel in front of it.

If we want to add *ing* we must double the consonant.

Add *ing* to the words on the left.
The first one is done for you.

run   running

A consonant...

hop

sit

shop

skip

...with one vowel in front of it.

step

grip

Double consonant.

shut

shopping

win

Fill in the missing words, using the *ing* words above.

Jasdeep is [   ] with her [   ] rope.

The builder is [   ] the hammer very tightly.

We must go because the shop is [   ] .

"Quick, catch the rabbit! He's [   ] away."

Here are some more words which follow the same spelling pattern:

hum   win   spin   swim   stop

In your book, add *ing* to each word - don't forget to double the consonant.
Write a sentence for each word that you have made.

© Andrew Brodie Publications ✓ PO Box 23, Wellington, Somerset, TA21 8YX ✓ www.andrewbrodie.co.uk

fold line

3. Copy each word in your best handwriting.

4. Look again at the first word, then fold the paper over it to cover it.

5. Write the word in COLUMN 3.

6. Check your spelling.

7. Now do the same for each word.

Learn, Write, Check.

Name:

Date:

1. Look carefully at each word.

2. Say the word out loud.

LEARN THE WORD	WRITE THEN COVER	WRITE THEN CHECK
run		
running		
hop		
hopping		
sit		
sitting		
skip		
skipping		
step		
stepping		
grip		
gripping		
shut		
shutting		
win		
winning		

© Andrew Brodie Publications ✓ PO Box 23, Wellington, Somerset, TA21 8YX ✓ www.andrewbrodie.co.uk

YEAR 3 Term 1

SET 4 Sheet A

hope	hoping
come	coming
smile	smiling
take	taking
care	caring
make	making
divide	dividing
stare	staring

© Andrew Brodie Publications ✓ PO Box 23, Wellington, Somerset, TA21 8YX ✓ www.andrewbrodie.co.uk

These words end with the letter e.

If we want to add **ing** we must take off the letter e.

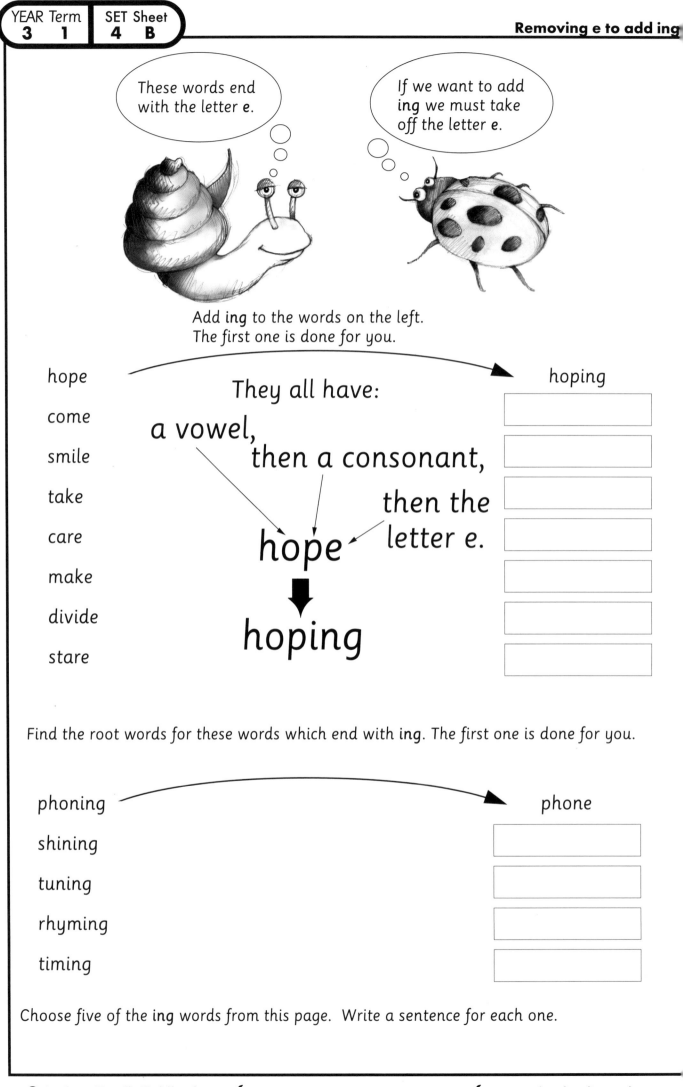

Add **ing** to the words on the left.
The first one is done for you.

hope → hoping

come

smile

take

care

make

divide

stare

They all have:

a vowel,

then a consonant,

then the letter e.

hope

↓

hoping

Find the root words for these words which end with **ing**. The first one is done for you.

phoning → phone

shining

tuning

rhyming

timing

Choose five of the **ing** words from this page. Write a sentence for each one.

© Andrew Brodie Publications ✓ PO Box 23, Wellington, Somerset, TA21 8YX ✓ www.andrewbrodie.co.uk

3. Copy each word in your best handwriting.

4. Look again at the first word, then fold the paper over it to cover it.

1. Look carefully at each word.

5. Write the word in COLUMN 3.

2. Say the word out loud.

6. Check your spelling.

7. Now do the same for each word.

Learn, Write, Check.

Name:

Date:

LEARN THE WORD	WRITE THEN COVER	WRITE THEN CHECK
hope		
hoping		
come		
coming		
smile		
smiling		
take		
taking		
care		
caring		
make		
making		
divide		
dividing		
stare		
staring		

© Andrew Brodie Publications ✓ PO Box 23, Wellington, Somerset, TA21 8YX ✓ www.andrewbrodie.co.uk

YEAR
3
Term
1

SET
5
Sheet
A

paddle	saddle
kettle	nettle
giggle	wiggle
middle	fiddle
muddle	puddle
rattle	cattle
nibble	little
puzzle	nuzzle

© Andrew Brodie Publications ✓ PO Box 23, Wellington, Somerset, TA21 8YX ✓ www.andrewbrodie.co.uk

Words which end with le...

...sometimes have double consonants in the middle.

kettle

↑

double t

paddle

↑

double d

giggle

↑

double g

Sort the words from the word bank.

WORD BANK

little   dazzle   giggle   nettle   nuzzle   kettle   middle

muddle   saddle   wobble   fiddle   puddle   puzzle

wiggle   paddle   dribble   nibble   rattle   cattle

double z

double d

double g

double b

double t

Can you think of any more words with double letters which end with le?

© Andrew Brodie Publications ✓ PO Box 23, Wellington, Somerset, TA21 8YX ✓ www.andrewbrodie.co.uk

fold line

1. Look carefully at each word.

2. Say the word out loud.

3. Copy each word in your best handwriting.

4. Look again at the first word, then fold the paper over it to cover it.

5. Write the word in COLUMN 3.

6. Check your spelling.

7. Now do the same for each word.

Learn, Write, Check.

Name:

Date:

LEARN THE WORD	WRITE THEN COVER	WRITE THEN CHECK
paddle		
saddle		
kettle		
nettle		
giggle		
wiggle		
middle		
fiddle		
muddle		
puddle		
rattle		
cattle		
nibble		
little		
puzzle		
nuzzle		

© Andrew Brodie Publications ✓ PO Box 23, Wellington, Somerset, TA21 8YX ✓ www.andrewbrodie.co.uk

tickle

trickle

pickle

prickle

cackle

crackle

chuckle

chuckling

tickling

trickling

prickling

crackling

tackle

tackling

knuckle

buckle

© Andrew Brodie Publications ✓ PO Box 23, Wellington, Somerset, TA21 8YX ✓ www.andrewbrodie.co.uk

Some words which end in le...

...can be changed to end with ing.

Add **ing** to the words on the left.
The first one is done for you.

tickle → tickling

trickle

pickle

prickle

crackle

tackle

chuckle

buckle

We remove the **e**

tickle

...and put **ing**.

tickling

Did you notice that all these words have **ck** before the ending **le**?

Choose the correct word to fill each gap:

I like [   ] with my cheese.

The water was [   ] slowly from the tap.

My friend was [   ] about the funny programme on television.

Now choose four words from this page.
Write a sentence for each of your four words.

© Andrew Brodie Publications ✓ PO Box 23, Wellington, Somerset, TA21 8YX ✓ www.andrewbrodie.co.uk

fold line

1. Look carefully at each word.

2. Say the word out loud.

3. Copy each word in your best handwriting.

4. Look again at the first word, then fold the paper over it to cover it.

5. Write the word in COLUMN 3.

6. Check your spelling.

7. Now do the same for each word.

Learn, Write, Check.

Name:

Date:

LEARN THE WORD	WRITE THEN COVER	WRITE THEN COVER
tickle		
trickle		
pickle		
prickle		
cackle		
crackle		
chuckle		
chuckling		
tickling		
trickling		
prickling		
crackling		
tackle		
tackling		
knuckle		
buckle		

© Andrew Brodie Publications ✓ PO Box 23, Wellington, Somerset, TA21 8YX ✓ www.andrewbrodie.co.uk

YEAR 3 Term 1 SET 7 Sheet A

able	table
cable	vegetable
valuable	reliable
probable	portable
terrible	horrible
visible	invisible
possible	impossible
responsible	sensible

© Andrew Brodie Publications ✓ PO Box 23, Wellington, Somerset, TA21 8YX ✓ www.andrewbrodie.co.uk

Words ending in able and ible.

Some words end in able and some words end in ible.

You need to look at the words very carefully.

WORD BANK

able   horrible   sensible   table   valuable   terrible
cable   vegetable   possible   portable   reliable   invisible
impossible   probable   visible   responsible

Sort the words from the word bank into two lists.

...able words	...ible words

Choose four of these words. Write a sentence for each one.

Some words can have **able** added to them to make new words. Look at these:

admire ➡ admirable

cure ➡ curable

Did you notice that the letter **e** at the end of **admire** and **cure** had been removed?

In your book, make new words by adding **able** to these words:

love

forgive

believe

move

remove

© Andrew Brodie Publications ✓ PO Box 23, Wellington, Somerset, TA21 8YX ✓ www.andrewbrodie.co.uk

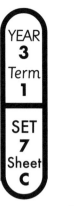

1. Look carefully at each word.

2. Say the word out loud.

fold line

3. Copy each word in your best handwriting.

4. Look again at the first word, then fold the paper over it to cover it.

5. Write the word in COLUMN 3.

6. Check your spelling.

7. Now do the same for each word.

Learn, Write, Check.

Name:

Date:

LEARN THE WORD	WRITE THEN COVER	WRITE THEN CHECK
able		
table		
cable		
vegetable		
valuable		
reliable		
probable		
portable		
terrible		
horrible		
visible		
invisible		
possible		
impossible		
responsible		
sensible		

© Andrew Brodie Publications ✓ PO Box 23, Wellington, Somerset, TA21 8YX ✓ www.andrewbrodie.co.uk

double

trouble

tumble

stumble

jumble

bumble

grumble

mumble

scramble

thimble

simple

example

sample

crumple

Bible

stable

© Andrew Brodie Publications ✓ PO Box 23, Wellington, Somerset, TA21 8YX ✓ www.andrewbrodie.co.uk

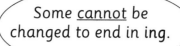

Some of the words in the word bank can be changed to end in ing.

Some <u>cannot</u> be changed to end in ing.

WORD BANK

double   crumple   thimble   fable   scramble   stable
simple   bumble   example   trouble   jumble   sample
mumble   tumble   grumble   stumble

Which of these words cannot be changed to end in **ing**?

Now sort all the words into the sets below.

Words which have letter **u** followed by letter **m**:

Words which have letter **o** followed by letter **u**:

Words which have a letter **m** but <u>not</u> a letter **u**:

Words that end in **ple**?

© Andrew Brodie Publications ✓ PO Box 23, Wellington, Somerset, TA21 8YX ✓ www.andrewbrodie.co.uk

fold line

3. Copy each word in your best handwriting.

4. Look again at the first word, then fold the paper over it to cover it.

1. Look carefully at each word.

5. Write the word in COLUMN 3.

2. Say the word out loud.

6. Check your spelling.

7. Now do the same for each word.

Learn, Write, Check.

YEAR 3 Term 1

SET 8 Sheet C

Name:

Date:

LEARN THE WORD	WRITE THEN COVER	WRITE THEN CHECK
double		
trouble		
tumble		
stumble		
jumble		
bumble		
grumble		
mumble		
scramble		
thimble		
simple		
example		
sample		
crumple		
Bible		
stable		

© Andrew Brodie Publications ✓ PO Box 23, Wellington, Somerset, TA21 8YX ✓ www.andrewbrodie.co.uk

● **Words ending in dle, gle or cle.**

Sh•

candle	handle
bundle	trundle
tingle	single
jingle	jungle
cycle	bicycle
uncle	circle
icicle	miracle
needle	bungle

© Andrew Brodie Publications ✓ PO Box 23, Wellington, Somerset, TA21 8YX ✓ www.andrewbrodie.co.uk

Look carefully at the words in the word bank.

Sort them into three sets.

WORD BANK

candle miracle bungle jungle trundle cycle single
uncle   handle   circle   bicycle   jingle   bundle
tingle   needle   icicle

...cle words	...dle words	...gle words

Read this sentence which has lots of **cle**, **dle** and **gle** words:

My uncle and I went into the jungle on our bicycles,
with bundles of food tied to the handlebars.

Try to write your own sentence, using as many of these words as you can.

© Andrew Brodie Publications ✓ PO Box 23, Wellington, Somerset, TA21 8YX ✓ www.andrewbrodie.co.uk

Learn, Write, Check.

1. Look carefully at each word.

2. Say the word out loud.

3. Copy each word in your best handwriting.

4. Look again at the first word, then fold the paper over it to cover it.

5. Write the word in COLUMN 3.

6. Check your spelling.

7. Now do the same for each word.

Name:

Date:

LEARN THE WORD	WRITE THEN COVER	WRITE THEN CHECK
candle		
handle		
bundle		
trundle		
tingle		
single		
jingle		
jungle		
cycle		
bicycle		
uncle		
circle		
icicle		
miracle		
needle		
bungle		

© Andrew Brodie Publications ✓ PO Box 23, Wellington, Somerset, TA21 8YX ✓ www.andrewbrodie.co.uk

happy	unhappy
tidy	untidy
lucky	unlucky
usual	unusual
zip	unzip
tie	untie
fair	unfair
kind	unkind

© Andrew Brodie Publications ✓ PO Box 23, Wellington, Somerset, TA21 8YX ✓ www.andrewbrodie.co.uk

We can make the opposites of some words...

...just by putting un at the start.

happy → unhappy

Add un to the words on the left.
The first one is done for you.

tidy

lucky

usual

zip

tie

fair

kind

Fill in the missing words.

I was very _____ when I got told off.

I had to _____ my coat because I was so hot.

The hoops were tied together so I had to _____ them.

You should not be _____ to other people.

Try to find three other words which can have **un** added at the start.
Write your pairs of words here:

© Andrew Brodie Publications ✓ PO Box 23, Wellington, Somerset, TA21 8YX ✓ www.andrewbrodie.co.uk

fold line

1. Look carefully at each word.

2. Say the word out loud.

3. Copy each word in your best handwriting.

4. Look again at the first word, then fold the paper over it to cover it.

5. Write the word in COLUMN 3.

6. Check your spelling.

7. Now do the same for each word.

Learn, Write, Check.

Name:

Date:

LEARN THE WORD	WRITE THEN COVER	WRITE THEN CHECK
happy		
unhappy		
tidy		
untidy		
lucky		
unlucky		
usual		
unusual		
zip		
unzip		
tie		
untie		
fair		
unfair		
kind		
unkind		

© Andrew Brodie Publications ✓ PO Box 23, Wellington, Somerset, TA21 8YX ✓ www.andrewbrodie.co.uk

YEAR
3
Term
1

SET
11
Sheet
A

code	decode
ice	de-ice
like	dislike
agree	disagree
appear	disappear
connect	disconnect
honest	dishonest
obey	disobey

© Andrew Brodie Publications ✓ PO Box 23, Wellington, Somerset, TA21 8YX ✓ www.andrewbrodie.co.uk

We can make the opposites of some words...

...by using the prefixes **de** or **dis**.

de

code → decode

ice → de-ice

Notice the use of a hyphen for this one.

dis

like → Add **dis** to the words on the left. The first one is done for you. → dislike

agree

appear

connect

honest

obey

Use the clues to help you to complete this crossword puzzle.

Clues across:
1. not telling the truth
2. We _____ the wires from a battery when we have finished using it.
3. to have a different opinion

Clues down:
4. to solve a message written in code
5. to vanish

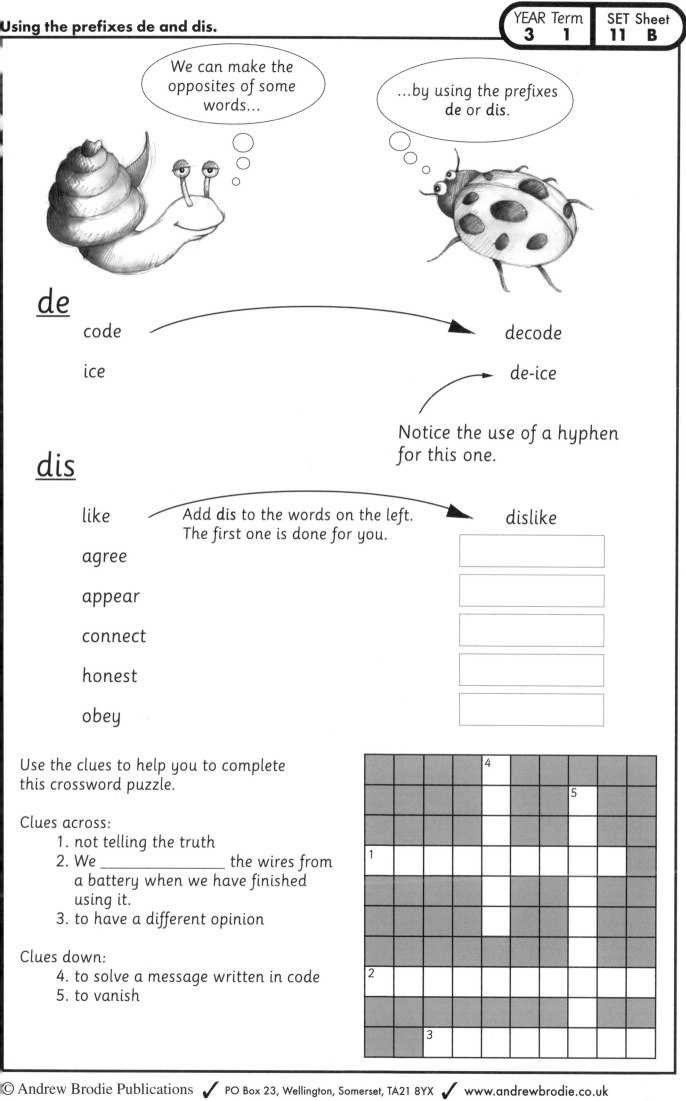

fold line

1. Look carefully at each word.

2. Say the word out loud.

3. Copy each word in your best handwriting.

4. Look again at the first word, then fold the paper over it to cover it.

5. Write the word in COLUMN 3.

6. Check your spelling.

7. Now do the same for each word.

Learn, Write, Check.

Name:

Date:

LEARN THE WORD	WRITE THEN COVER	WRITE THEN CHECK
code		
decode		
ice		
de-ice		
like		
dislike		
agree		
disagree		
appear		
disappear		
connect		
disconnect		
honest		
dishonest		
obey		
disobey		

© Andrew Brodie Publications ✓ PO Box 23, Wellington, Somerset, TA21 8YX ✓ www.andrewbrodie.co.uk

build	rebuild
visit	revisit
play	replay
write	rewrite
cycle	recycle
place	replace
turn	return
prepare	prefix

© Andrew Brodie Publications ✓ PO Box 23, Wellington, Somerset, TA21 8YX ✓ www.andrewbrodie.co.uk

The prefix re...

...usually means to do something again.

build   Add **re** to the words on the left.   rebuild
The first one is done for you.

visit

play

write

cycle

place

turn

These two words start with **pre**:

prepare   prefix

Can you think of any other words which start with **pre**?

Use a dictionary to help you find them.

3. Copy each word in your best handwriting.

4. Look again at the first word, then fold the paper over it to cover it.

1. Look carefully at each word.

5. Write the word in COLUMN 3.

2. Say the word out loud.

6. Check your spelling.

7. Now do the same for each word.

Learn, Write, Check.

Name:

Date:

LEARN THE WORD	WRITE THEN COVER	WRITE THEN CHECK
build		
rebuild		
visit		
revisit		
play		
replay		
write		
rewrite		
cycle		
recycle		
place		
replace		
turn		
return		
prepare		
prefix		

© Andrew Brodie Publications ✓ PO Box 23, Wellington, Somerset, TA21 8YX ✓ www.andrewbrodie.co.uk

YEAR
3
Term
2

SET
13
Sheet
A

fast	slow
faster	slower
fastest	slowest
quick	cold
quicker	colder
quickest	coldest

long

longer	longest

© Andrew Brodie Publications ✓ PO Box 23, Wellington, Somerset, TA21 8YX ✓ www.andrewbrodie.co.uk

We can change the meaning of some words...

...just by putting a suffix at the end.

Kim's hair is quite long

Sam's hair is longer than Kim's
↑
we have added the suffix **er**

Jasdeep's hair is longest of all.
↑
we have added the suffix **est**

Fill in the gaps

long ⟶ longer ⟶ longest

fast ⟶ [   ] ⟶ [   ]

slow ⟶ [   ] ⟶ [   ]

quick ⟶ [   ] ⟶ [   ]

cold ⟶ [   ] ⟶ [   ]

Use fast, faster and fastest to write three sentences.

© Andrew Brodie Publications ✓ PO Box 23, Wellington, Somerset, TA21 8YX ✓ www.andrewbrodie.co.uk

fold line

Learn, Write, Check.

1. Look carefully at each word.

2. Say the word out loud.

3. Copy each word in your best handwriting.

4. Look again at the first word, then fold the paper over it to cover it.

5. Write the word in COLUMN 3.

6. Check your spelling.

7. Now do the same for each word.

Name:

Date:

LEARN THE WORD	WRITE THEN COVER	WRITE THEN CHECK
fast		
faster		
fastest		
slow		
slower		
slowest		
quick		
quicker		
quickest		
cold		
colder		
coldest		
long		
longer		
longest		

© Andrew Brodie Publications ✓ PO Box 23, Wellington, Somerset, TA21 8YX ✓ www.andrewbrodie.co.uk

late

close

later

closer

latest

closest

wide

safe

wider

safer

widest

safest

nice

nicer

nicest

© Andrew Brodie Publications ✓ PO Box 23, Wellington, Somerset, TA21 8YX ✓ www.andrewbrodie.co.uk

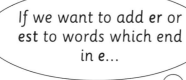

*If we want to add **er** or **est** to words which end in e...*

...we have to remove the e first.

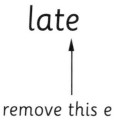

Look:

late   later   latest

remove this e   then add er...   ...or est.

Fill in the gaps:

late	→	later	→	latest
close	→		→	
wide	→		→	
safe	→		→	
nice	→		→	

Solve the puzzle, using these clues:

Clues across:
1. begins with n and ends with r
2. begins with c and ends with t
3. begins with s and ends with t
4. begins with w and ends with r

Clues down:

5. begins with l and ends with r

6. begins with w and ends with t

7. begins with l and ends with t

8. begins with n and ends with t

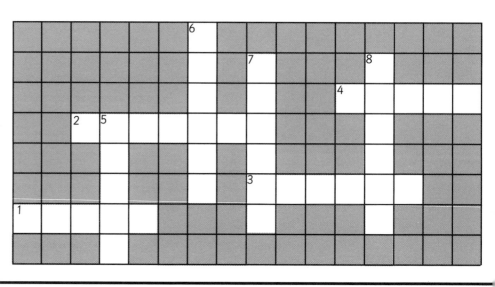

3. Copy each word in your best handwriting.

4. Look again at the first word, then fold the paper over it to cover it.

Learn, Write, Check.

1. Look carefully at each word.

2. Say the word out loud.

5. Write the word in COLUMN 3.

6. Check your spelling.

7. Now do the same for each word.

Name:

Date:

LEARN THE WORD	WRITE THEN COVER	WRITE THEN CHECK
late		
later		
latest		
close		
closer		
closest		
wide		
wider		
widest		
safe		
safer		
safest		
nice		
nicer		
nicest		

© Andrew Brodie Publications ✓ PO Box 23, Wellington, Somerset, TA21 8YX ✓ www.andrewbrodie.co.uk

YEAR
3
Term
2

SET
15
Sheet
A

big

fit

bigger

fitter

biggest

fittest

sad

good

sadder

better

saddest

best

bad

worse

worst

© Andrew Brodie Publications ✓ PO Box 23, Wellington, Somerset, TA21 8YX ✓ www.andrewbrodie.co.uk

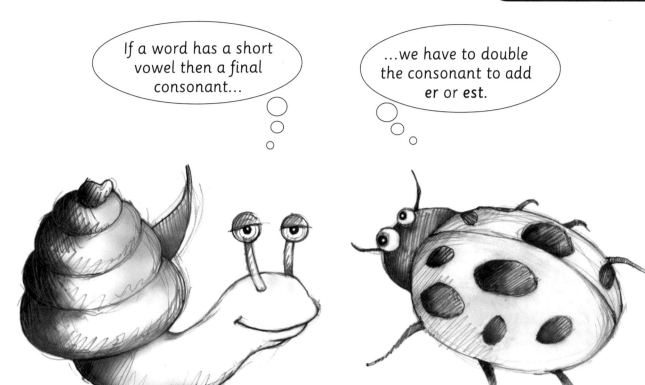

If a word has a short vowel then a final consonant...

...we have to double the consonant to add **er** or **est**.

Look:

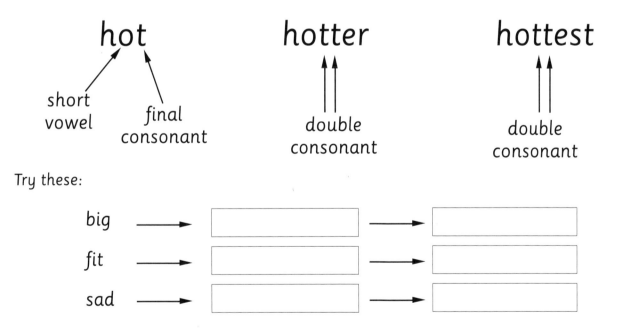

hot

short vowel   final consonant

hotter

double consonant

hottest

double consonant

Try these:

big ⟶ [   ] ⟶ [   ]

fit ⟶ [   ] ⟶ [   ]

sad ⟶ [   ] ⟶ [   ]

Now look at these words which behave very strangely.

good ⟶ better ⟶ best

bad ⟶ worse ⟶ worst

Write three sentences using good, better and best.

© Andrew Brodie Publications ✓ PO Box 23, Wellington, Somerset, TA21 8YX ✓ www.andrewbrodie.co.uk

fold line

1. Look carefully at each word.

2. Say the word out loud.

3. Copy each word in your best handwriting.

4. Look again at the first word, then fold the paper over it to cover it.

5. Write the word in COLUMN 3.

6. Check your spelling.

7. Now do the same for each word.

Learn, Write, Check.

Name:

Date:

LEARN THE WORD	WRITE THEN COVER	WRITE THEN CHECK
big		
bigger		
biggest		
fit		
fitter		
fittest		
sad		
sadder		
saddest		
good		
better		
best		
bad		
worse		
worst		

© Andrew Brodie Publications ✓ PO Box 23, Wellington, Somerset, TA21 8YX ✓ www.andrewbrodie.co.uk

happy	foggy
happier	foggier
happiest	foggiest
wavy	funny
wavier	funnier
waviest	funniest

lucky

luckier	luckiest

© Andrew Brodie Publications ✓ PO Box 23, Wellington, Somerset, TA21 8YX ✓ www.andrewbrodie.co.uk

Look:

happy   happier   happiest

ends in a y   change the y to an i

Try these:

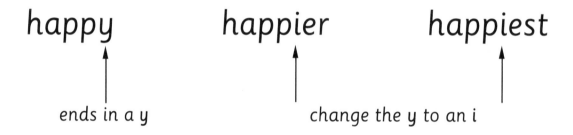

foggy ⟶ ☐ ⟶ ☐

wavy ⟶ ☐ ⟶ ☐

funny ⟶ ☐ ⟶ ☐

lucky ⟶ ☐ ⟶ ☐

In your book, write three sentences using funny, funnier and funniest.

Now write three sentences using lucky, luckier and luckiest.

© Andrew Brodie Publications ✓ PO Box 23, Wellington, Somerset, TA21 8YX ✓ www.andrewbrodie.co.uk

fold line

Learn, Write, Check.

1. Look carefully at each word.

2. Say the word out loud.

3. Copy each word in your best handwriting.

4. Look again at the first word, then fold the paper over it to cover it.

5. Write the word in COLUMN 3.

6. Check your spelling.

7. Now do the same for each word.

Name:

Date:

LEARN THE WORD	WRITE THEN COVER	WRITE THEN CHECK
happy		
happier		
happiest		
foggy		
foggier		
foggiest		
wavy		
wavier		
waviest		
funny		
funnier		
funniest		
lucky		
luckier		
luckiest		

© Andrew Brodie Publications ✓ PO Box 23, Wellington, Somerset, TA21 8YX ✓ www.andrewbrodie.co.uk

● **Changing words by adding y.**

mess	messy
ink	inky
full	fully
fuss	fussy
mood	moody
sleep	sleepy
dream	dreamy
cheek	cheeky

© Andrew Brodie Publications ✓ PO Box 23, Wellington, Somerset, TA21 8YX ✓ www.andrewbrodie.co.uk

If words have two consonants at the end...

...or two vowels before a final consonant...

... it's easy to add y.

Look:

mess ⟶ **messy**

two consonants

Just add y

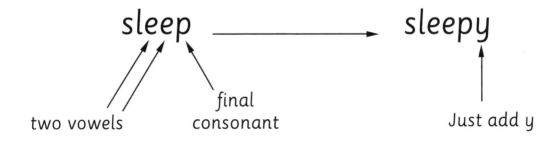

sleep ⟶ **sleepy**

two vowels   final consonant

Just add y

Fill the gaps, then add two more words with the same pattern to each column.

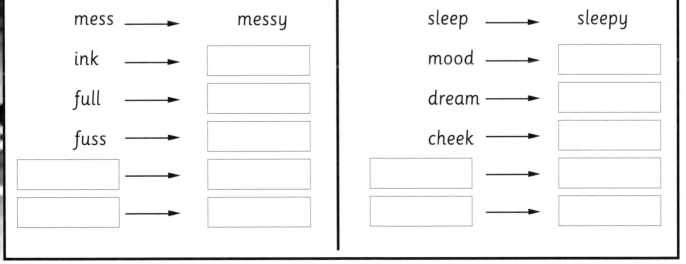

mess ⟶ messy

ink ⟶

full ⟶

fuss ⟶

⟶

⟶

sleep ⟶ sleepy

mood ⟶

dream ⟶

cheek ⟶

⟶

⟶

© Andrew Brodie Publications ✓ PO Box 23, Wellington, Somerset, TA21 8YX ✓ www.andrewbrodie.co.uk

Learn, Write, Check.

fold line

1. Look carefully at each word.

2. Say the word out loud.

3. Copy each word in your best handwriting.

4. Look again at the first word, then fold the paper over it to cover it.

5. Write the word in COLUMN 3.

6. Check your spelling.

7. Now do the same for each word.

Name:

Date:

LEARN THE WORD	WRITE THEN COVER	WRITE THEN CHECK
mess		
messy		
ink		
inky		
full		
fully		
fuss		
fussy		
mood		
moody		
sleep		
sleepy		
dream		
dreamy		
cheek		
cheeky		

© Andrew Brodie Publications ✓ PO Box 23, Wellington, Somerset, TA21 8YX ✓ www.andrewbrodie.co.uk

YEAR **3** Term **2**

SET **18** Sheet **A**

fun	funny
run	runny
sun	sunny
tin	tinny
pop	poppy
dot	dotty
rat	ratty
bat	batty

© Andrew Brodie Publications ✓ PO Box 23, Wellington, Somerset, TA21 8YX ✓ www.andrewbrodie.co.uk

Is the sun out today?

No, it's not sunny.

Look:

sun ⟶ sunny

short vowel   final consonant

two consonants

Fill the gaps.

sun ⟶ sunny

fun ⟶ [ ]

run ⟶ [ ]

tin ⟶ [ ]

pop ⟶ [ ]

dot ⟶ [ ]

rat ⟶ [ ]

bat ⟶ [ ]

Find the correct words to fill these gaps.

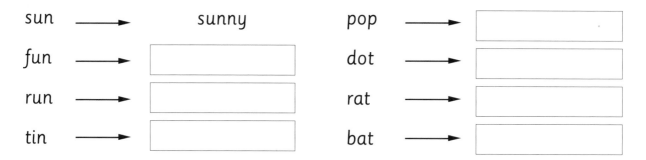

He's in a bad mood. He's very [ ] .

A [ ] is a pretty, red flower.

Sam had [ ] at his party.

The jokes were very [ ] .

Now choose four other words to use in sentences.

fold line

3. Copy each word in your best handwriting.

4. Look again at the first word, then fold the paper over it to cover it.

1. Look carefully at each word.

2. Say the word out loud.

5. Write the word in COLUMN 3.

6. Check your spelling.

7. Now do the same for each word.

Learn, Write, Check.

Name:

Date:

LEARN THE WORD	WRITE THEN COVER	WRITE THEN CHECK
fun		
funny		
run		
runny		
sun		
sunny		
tin		
tinny		
pop		
poppy		
dot		
dotty		
rat		
ratty		
bat		
batty		

© Andrew Brodie Publications ✓ PO Box 23, Wellington, Somerset, TA21 8YX ✓ www.andrewbrodie.co.uk

YEAR 3 Term **2**
SET **19** Sheet **A**

laze	lazy
ease	easy
smoke	smoky
shine	shiny
rose	rosy
stone	stony
breeze	breezy
bone	bony

© Andrew Brodie Publications ✓ PO Box 23, Wellington, Somerset, TA21 8YX ✓ www.andrewbrodie.co.uk

When words end in e...

...we take off the e to add y.

Look:

smoke ——————→ smoky

Follow the rule to fill these gaps.

smoke ——→ smoky   rose ——→ [   ]

laze ——→ [   ]   stone ——→ [   ]

ease ——→ [   ]   breeze ——→ [   ]

shine ——→ [   ]   bone ——→ [   ]

Find the correct words to fill these gaps.

We were coughing because the fire was [   ].

Sometimes I just [   ] about doing nothing.

This work is [   ].

My new pound coin is very [   ].

Choose four words from this page. Write a sentence for each one.

© Andrew Brodie Publications ✔ PO Box 23, Wellington, Somerset, TA21 8YX ✔ www.andrewbrodie.co.uk

Learn, Write, Check.

1. Look carefully at each word.

2. Say the word out loud.

fold line

3. Copy each word in your best handwriting.

4. Look again at the first word, then fold the paper over it to cover it.

5. Write the word in COLUMN 3.

6. Check your spelling.

7. Now do the same for each word.

Name:

Date:

LEARN THE WORD	WRITE THEN COVER	WRITE THEN CHECK
laze		
lazy		
ease		
easy		
smoke		
smoky		
shine		
shiny		
rose		
rosy		
stone		
stony		
breeze		
breezy		
bone		
bony		

© Andrew Brodie Publications ✓ PO Box 23, Wellington, Somerset, TA21 8YX ✓ www.andrewbrodie.co.uk

boy	boys
girl	girls
table	tables
book	books
desk	desks
time	times
window	windows
house	houses

© Andrew Brodie Publications ✓ PO Box 23, Wellington, Somerset, TA21 8YX ✓ www.andrewbrodie.co.uk

With some words...

...you just need to add s to make them plural.

Look:

one girl ⟶ two girls

Just add s

These words follow the same rule.

table ⟶ [　　　　]　　　book ⟶ [　　　　]

desk ⟶ [　　　　]　　　time ⟶ [　　　　]

window ⟶ [　　　　]　　　house ⟶ [　　　　]

Find some more words which follow this rule.

boy	⟶	boys
	⟶	
	⟶	

	⟶	
	⟶	
	⟶	

© Andrew Brodie Publications ✓ PO Box 23, Wellington, Somerset, TA21 8YX ✓ www.andrewbrodie.co.uk

Learn, Write, Check.

fold line

1. Look carefully at each word.

2. Say the word out loud.

3. Copy each word in your best handwriting.

4. Look again at the first word, then fold the paper over it to cover it.

5. Write the word in COLUMN 3.

6. Check your spelling.

7. Now do the same for each word.

Name:

Date:

LEARN THE WORD	WRITE THEN COVER	WRITE THEN CHECK
boy		
boys		
girl		
girls		
table		
tables		
book		
books		
desk		
desks		
time		
times		
window		
windows		
house		
houses		

© Andrew Brodie Publications ✓ PO Box 23, Wellington, Somerset, TA21 8YX ✓ www.andrewbrodie.co.uk

● **Some words need es to make them plural.**

YEAR 3 Term 2 SET 21 Sheet A

catch	catches
match	matches
push	pushes
brush	brushes
blush	blushes
fox	foxes
box	boxes
church	churches

© Andrew Brodie Publications ✓ PO Box 23, Wellington, Somerset, TA21 8YX ✓ www.andrewbrodie.co.uk

Some words which are singular have one syllable.

When they are made plural they have two syllables.

Look:　fox $\longrightarrow$ foxes

Say this word out loud.
It has one syllable.

Say this word out loud.
It has two syllables.

Make the singular words plural by adding **es**.

catch $\longrightarrow$ [　　　　]

match $\longrightarrow$ [　　　　]

push $\longrightarrow$ [　　　　]

brush $\longrightarrow$ [　　　　]

blush $\longrightarrow$ [　　　　]

fox $\longrightarrow$ [　　　　]

box $\longrightarrow$ [　　　　]

church $\longrightarrow$ [　　　　]

Four words in this word bank follow the **es** rule.

WORD BANK

school　　book　　watch　　pocket　　ditch　　fax

fizz　　ruler　　pencil

Find the four words and write the singular and plural version of each word.

[　　　] $\longrightarrow$ [　　　]　　[　　　] $\longrightarrow$ [　　　]

[　　　] $\longrightarrow$ [　　　]　　[　　　] $\longrightarrow$ [　　　]

© Andrew Brodie Publications ✓ PO Box 23, Wellington, Somerset, TA21 8YX ✓ www.andrewbrodie.co.uk

Learn, Write, Check.

1. Look carefully at each word.

2. Say the word out loud.

fold line

3. Copy each word in your best handwriting.

4. Look again at the first word, then fold the paper over it to cover it.

5. Write the word in COLUMN 3.

6. Check your spelling.

7. Now do the same for each word.

Name:

Date:

LEARN THE WORD	WRITE THEN COVER	WRITE THEN CHECK
catch		
catches		
match		
matches		
push		
pushes		
brush		
brushes		
blush		
blushes		
fox		
foxes		
box		
boxes		
church		
churches		

© Andrew Brodie Publications ✓ PO Box 23, Wellington, Somerset, TA21 8YX ✓ www.andrewbrodie.co.uk

● **Making plurals for words ending in a vowel then y.**

day	days
key	keys
tray	trays
monkey	monkeys
play	plays
holiday	holidays
birthday	birthdays
buy	buys

© Andrew Brodie Publications ✓ PO Box 23, Wellington, Somerset, TA21 8YX ✓ www.andrewbrodie.co.uk

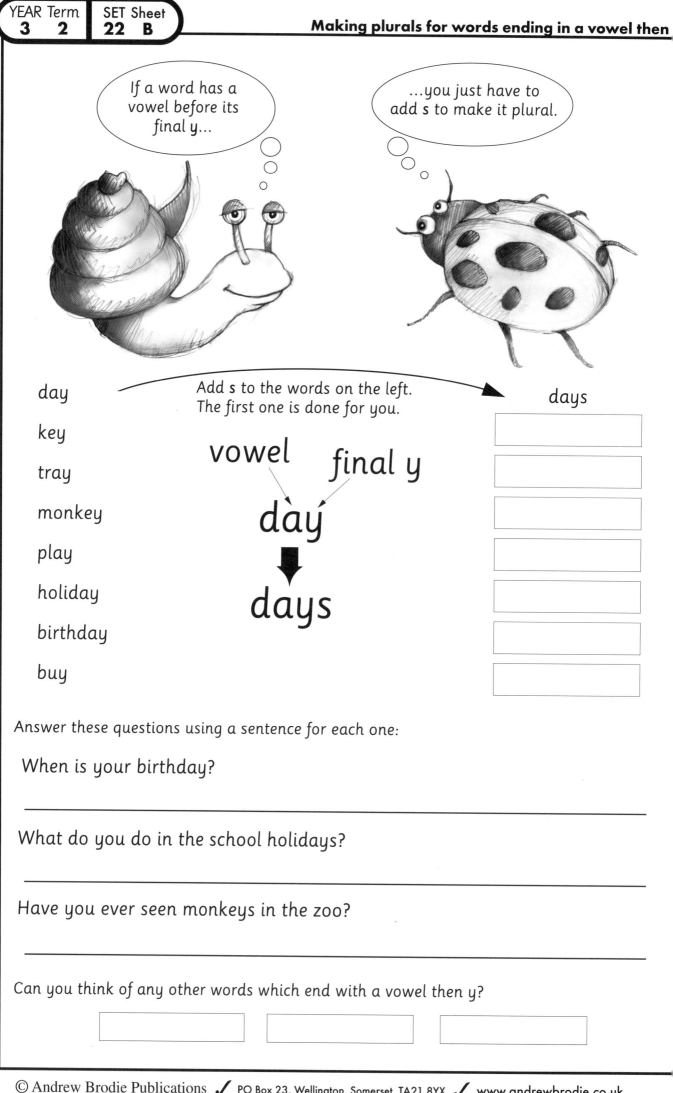

If a word has a vowel before its final y...

...you just have to add s to make it plural.

day

key

tray

monkey

play

holiday

birthday

buy

Add s to the words on the left.
The first one is done for you.

vowel   final y

day

days

days

Answer these questions using a sentence for each one:

When is your birthday?

_____

What do you do in the school holidays?

_____

Have you ever seen monkeys in the zoo?

_____

Can you think of any other words which end with a vowel then y?

fold line

1. Look carefully at each word.

2. Say the word out loud.

3. Copy each word in your best handwriting.

4. Look again at the first word, then fold the paper over it to cover it.

5. Write the word in COLUMN 3.

6. Check your spelling.

7. Now do the same for each word.

Learn, Write, Check.

Name:

Date:

LEARN THE WORD	WRITE THEN COVER	WRITE THEN CHECK
day		
days		
key		
keys		
tray		
trays		
monkey		
monkeys		
play		
plays		
holiday		
holidays		
birthday		
birthdays		
buy		
buys		

© Andrew Brodie Publications ✓ PO Box 23, Wellington, Somerset, TA21 8YX ✓ www.andrewbrodie.co.uk

YEAR 3
Term 2
SET 23
Sheet A

baby	babies
lady	ladies
puppy	puppies
pony	ponies
party	parties
penny	pennies
hobby	hobbies
fly	flies

© Andrew Brodie Publications ✓ PO Box 23, Wellington, Somerset, TA21 8YX ✓ www.andrewbrodie.co.uk

If a word has a consonant before its final y...

...you have to replace the y with an i, then add **es**.

Make the singular words on the left into plural words.
The first one is done for you.

baby   babies

lady

puppy

consonant   final y

pony

party

pony

penny

hobby

ponies

fly

replace the y with an i...

...then add es

Find the correct words to fill these gaps.

The dog had six _____ .

Two of my friends had birthdays so I went to both _____ .

There were lots of _____ by the horse's face.

Fill the gap then answer this question:

How many _____ make one pound?

© Andrew Brodie Publications ✓ PO Box 23, Wellington, Somerset, TA21 8YX ✓ www.andrewbrodie.co.uk

Learn, Write, Check.

1. Look carefully at each word.

2. Say the word out loud.

fold line

3. Copy each word in your best handwriting.

4. Look again at the first word, then fold the paper over it to cover it.

5. Write the word in COLUMN 3.

6. Check your spelling.

7. Now do the same for each word.

Name:

Date:

LEARN THE WORD	WRITE THEN COVER	WRITE THEN CHECK
baby		
babies		
lady		
ladies		
puppy		
puppies		
pony		
ponies		
party		
parties		
penny		
pennies		
hobby		
hobbies		
fly		
flies		

© Andrew Brodie Publications ✓ PO Box 23, Wellington, Somerset, TA21 8YX ✓ www.andrewbrodie.co.uk

man	men
woman	women
child	children
tooth	teeth
mouse	mice
goose	geese
calf	calves
wolf	wolves

© Andrew Brodie Publications ✓ PO Box 23, Wellington, Somerset, TA21 8YX ✓ www.andrewbrodie.co.uk

The plural of house is houses.

But the plural of mouse is <u>not</u> mouses!

Find the plurals for each of these singular words. Use the words in the word bank.

man ⟶ [ ]

woman ⟶ [ ]

child ⟶ [ ]

tooth ⟶ [ ]

goose ⟶ [ ]

foot ⟶ [ ]

mouse ⟶ [ ]

headlouse ⟶ [ ]

calf ⟶ [ ]

half ⟶ [ ]

wolf ⟶ [ ]

shelf ⟶ [ ]

WORD BANK

children   geese   mice   halves   teeth
women   wolves   headlice   men   feet
calves   shelves

Write a sentence to answer this question:

How many teeth have you got?

_____

Now choose four more words from this page. Write a question sentence for each one.

© Andrew Brodie Publications ✓ PO Box 23, Wellington, Somerset, TA21 8YX ✓ www.andrewbrodie.co.uk

Learn, Write, Check.

1. Look carefully at each word.

2. Say the word out loud.

fold line

3. Copy each word in your best handwriting.

4. Look again at the first word, then fold the paper over it to cover it.

5. Write the word in COLUMN 3.

6. Check your spelling.

7. Now do the same for each word.

Name:

Date:

LEARN THE WORD	WRITE THEN COVER	WRITE THEN CHECK
man		
men		
woman		
women		
child		
children		
tooth		
teeth		
mouse		
mice		
goose		
geese		
calf		
calves		
wolf		
wolves		

© Andrew Brodie Publications ✓ PO Box 23, Wellington, Somerset, TA21 8YX ✓ www.andrewbrodie.co.uk

● **Silent letters.**

knee	kneel
knife	knives
know	knock
gnat	gnome
write	wrist
wrap	wrapping
when	where
honest	rhyme

© Andrew Brodie Publications ✓ PO Box 23, Wellington, Somerset, TA21 8YX ✓ www.andrewbrodie.co.uk

Some words include letters which make no sound at all.

We call these silent letters.

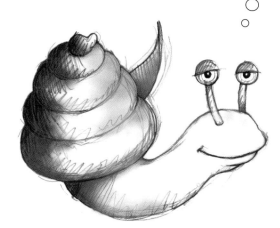

WORD BANK

rhyme   knives   kneel   gnome   wrap   knee

honest   where   knock   wrapping   knife

write   gnat   know   wrist   when

In the word bank:

four words have silent h
four words have silent w
two words have silent g
six words have silent k.

Write the words in the correct list below. See if you can think of an extra word for each list.

silent h	silent w	silent g	silent k

© Andrew Brodie Publications ✓ PO Box 23, Wellington, Somerset, TA21 8YX ✓ www.andrewbrodie.co.uk

1. Look carefully at each word.

2. Say the word out loud.

fold line

3. Copy each word in your best handwriting.

4. Look again at the first word, then fold the paper over it to cover it.

5. Write the word in COLUMN 3.

6. Check your spelling.

7. Now do the same for each word.

Learn, Write, Check.

Name:

Date:

LEARN THE WORD	WRITE THEN COVER	WRITE THEN CHECK
knee		
kneel		
knife		
knives		
know		
knock		
gnat		
gnome		
write		
wrist		
wrap		
wrapping		
when		
where		
honest		
rhyme		

© Andrew Brodie Publications ✔ PO Box 23, Wellington, Somerset, TA21 8YX ✔ www.andrewbrodie.co.uk

comb

bomb

thumb

crumb

lamb

numb

calf

calves

half

halves

calm

palm

could

should

would

© Andrew Brodie Publications ✓ PO Box 23, Wellington, Somerset, TA21 8YX ✓ www.andrewbrodie.co.uk

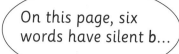

On this page, six words have silent b...

...and nine words have silent l.

WORD BANK

halves   could   crumb   palm   should   bomb

half   calm   calf   comb   thumb

calves   would   lamb   numb

Sort the words in the word bank into two sets.

<u>silent b words</u>

<u>silent l words</u>

Write a sentence which includes the words:

lamb   calf

_____

_____

Now try writing a sentence which includes five words with silent letters. This could be tricky!

_____

_____

fold line

3. Copy each word in your best handwriting.

4. Look again at the first word, then fold the paper over it to cover it.

1. Look carefully at each word.

2. Say the word out loud.

5. Write the word in COLUMN 3.

6. Check your spelling.

7. Now do the same for each word.

Learn, Write, Check.

Name:

Date:

LEARN THE WORD	WRITE THEN COVER	WRITE THEN CHECK
comb		
bomb		
thumb		
crumb		
lamb		
numb		
calf		
calves		
half		
halves		
calm		
palm		
could		
should		
would		

© Andrew Brodie Publications ✓ PO Box 23, Wellington, Somerset, TA21 8YX ✓ www.andrewbrodie.co.uk

YEAR
3
Term
2

SET
27
Sheet
A

play	playground
motor	motorway
bed	bedroom
every	everybody
everyone	everything
some	somebody
someone	something
somewhere	sometimes

© Andrew Brodie Publications ✓ PO Box 23, Wellington, Somerset, TA21 8YX ✓ www.andrewbrodie.co.uk

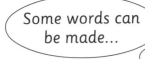

Some words can be made...

...by joining two other words together.

We have started this chart for you. Can you finish it by filling in the gaps?

every	⟶	body	⟶	everybody
bed	⟶	room	⟶	☐
every	⟶	☐	⟶	everything
some	⟶	where	⟶	☐
some	⟶	☐	⟶	somebody
some	⟶	thing	⟶	☐
every	⟶	one	⟶	☐
play	⟶	ground	⟶	☐
some	⟶	☐	⟶	someone
some	⟶	times	⟶	☐
motor	⟶	way	⟶	☐

Words which are made by joining others together are called **compound** words.
Can you think of four other compound words?

☐ ☐ ☐ ☐

© Andrew Brodie Publications ✓ PO Box 23, Wellington, Somerset, TA21 8YX ✓ www.andrewbrodie.co.uk

fold line

1. Look carefully at each word.

2. Say the word out loud.

3. Copy each word in your best handwriting.

4. Look again at the first word, then fold the paper over it to cover it.

5. Write the word in COLUMN 3.

6. Check your spelling.

7. Now do the same for each word.

Learn, Write, Check.

Name:

Date:

LEARN THE WORD	WRITE THEN COVER	WRITE THEN CHECK
play		
playground		
motor		
motorway		
bed		
bedroom		
every		
everybody		
everyone		
everything		
some		
somebody		
someone		
something		
somewhere		
sometimes		

© Andrew Brodie Publications ✓ PO Box 23, Wellington, Somerset, TA21 8YX ✓ www.andrewbrodie.co.uk

pan	pancake
week	weekend
goal	goalkeeper
break	breakfast
stairs	upstairs
downstairs	any
anybody	anyone
anything	anywhere

© Andrew Brodie Publications ✓ PO Box 23, Wellington, Somerset, TA21 8YX ✓ www.andrewbrodie.co.uk

How many words can you think of which end with **body** ?

I can think of: **anybody**, **nobody**, **somebody** and **everybody**.

START WORDS

pan   down   up   any
goal   week   break
some

END WORDS

one   stairs   fast   cake
thing   keeper   body
where   end   times

Make some compound words using the START WORDS and END WORDS above.
Some of them can be used more than once.

START WORD	END WORD	COMPOUND WORD

Learn, Write, Check.

fold line

3. Copy each word in your best handwriting.

4. Look again at the first word, then fold the paper over it to cover it.

5. Write the word in COLUMN 3.

6. Check your spelling.

7. Now do the same for each word.

1. Look carefully at each word.

2. Say the word out loud.

Name:

Date:

LEARN THE WORD	WRITE THEN COVER	WRITE THEN CHECK
pan		
pancake		
week		
weekend		
goal		
goalkeeper		
break		
breakfast		
stairs		
upstairs		
downstairs		
any		
anybody		
anyone		
anything		
anywhere		

© Andrew Brodie Publications ✓ PO Box 23, Wellington, Somerset, TA21 8YX ✓ www.andrewbrodie.co.uk

YEAR
3
Term
2

SET
29
Sheet
A

love	lovely
nice	nicely
like	likely
safe	safely
real	really
usual	usually
regular	regularly
proper	properly

© Andrew Brodie Publications ✓ PO Box 23, Wellington, Somerset, TA21 8YX ✓ www.andrewbrodie.co.uk

Suffixes are extra parts added to the ends of some words.

For example, we can add ly to the word **love** and make **lovely**.

Add ly to these words to make new words.

love   ⟶

nice   ⟶

like   ⟶

safe   ⟶

real   ⟶

usual   ⟶

regular   ⟶

proper   ⟶

Check that your words look exactly like these:

lovely   nicely   likely   safely   really

usually   regularly   properly

Choose one of these words to fill the gap in each of these sentences.

Rain in January is quite   .

Swimming is   good fun.

You must cross the road   .

Now write three sentences of your own. Use a word which ends in ly in each sentence.

© Andrew Brodie Publications ✓ PO Box 23, Wellington, Somerset, TA21 8YX ✓ www.andrewbrodie.co.uk

fold line

1. Look carefully at each word.

2. Say the word out loud.

3. Copy each word in your best handwriting.

4. Look again at the first word, then fold the paper over it to cover it.

5. Write the word in COLUMN 3.

6. Check your spelling.

7. Now do the same for each word.

Learn, Write, Check.

Name:

Date:

LEARN THE WORD	WRITE THEN COVER	WRITE THEN CHECK
love		
lovely		
nice		
nicely		
like		
likely		
safe		
safely		
real		
really		
usual		
usually		
regular		
regularly		
proper		
properly		

© Andrew Brodie Publications ✓ PO Box 23, Wellington, Somerset, TA21 8YX ✓ www.andrewbrodie.co.uk

hope	hopeful
care	careful
pain	painful
use	useful
wonder	wonderful
cheer	cheerful
beauty	beautiful
till	until

© Andrew Brodie Publications ✓ PO Box 23, Wellington, Somerset, TA21 8YX ✓ www.andrewbrodie.co.uk

Some words can have the suffix *ful* added to them.

Careful means full of care.

full of care

double l

➡

careful

single l

Add the suffix *ful* to these words.

hope ⟶ [ ]   pain ⟶ [ ]

use ⟶ [ ]   wonder ⟶ [ ]

cheer ⟶ [ ]   care ⟶ [ ]

Look carefully at this one:

beauty   ➡   beautiful

letter y

we have replaced the y with an i

Practise writing beauty and beautiful.

[ ]   [ ]

<u>A different ending:</u>
Read these two sentences:

I stayed out till late.

I stayed out until 10 o'clock.

till   ➡   until

double l

single l

Write two sentences including the words till and until.

© Andrew Brodie Publications ✓ PO Box 23, Wellington, Somerset, TA21 8YX ✓ www.andrewbrodie.co.uk

Learn, Write, Check.

fold line

3. Copy each word in your best handwriting.

4. Look again at the first word, then fold the paper over it to cover it.

1. Look carefully at each word.

5. Write the word in COLUMN 3.

2. Say the word out loud.

6. Check your spelling.

7. Now do the same for each word.

Name:

Date:

LEARN THE WORD	WRITE THEN COVER	WRITE THEN CHECK
hope		
hopeful		
care		
careful		
pain		
painful		
use		
useful		
wonder		
wonderful		
cheer		
cheerful		
beauty		
beautiful		
till		
until		

© Andrew Brodie Publications ✓ PO Box 23, Wellington, Somerset, TA21 8YX ✓ www.andrewbrodie.co.uk

YEAR
3
Term
2

SET
31
Sheet
A

hope	hopeless
care	careless
pain	painless
use	useless
home	homeless
speech	speechless
end	endless
harm	harmless

© Andrew Brodie Publications ✓ PO Box 23, Wellington, Somerset, TA21 8YX ✓ www.andrewbrodie.co.uk

Some words can have the suffix less added to them.

Harmless means there is no harm.

Add the suffix less to these words.

hope ⟶ [ ]

pain ⟶ [ ]

home ⟶ [ ]

end ⟶ [ ]

care ⟶ [ ]

use ⟶ [ ]

speech ⟶ [ ]

harm ⟶ [ ]

Fill in the missing words.

Some snakes can bite but some are [ ] .

Usually, having an injection is [ ] .

Sometimes I make [ ] mistakes.

Try to complete this crossword:

CLUES ACROSS
1. Not speaking at all.
3. No hope.
4. Without end.
5. No pain.

CLUES DOWN
2. Not careful
3. Not dangerous.

1. Look carefully at each word.

2. Say the word out loud.

fold line

3. Copy each word in your best handwriting.

4. Look again at the first word, then fold the paper over it to cover it.

5. Write the word in COLUMN 3.

6. Check your spelling.

7. Now do the same for each word.

Learn, Write, Check.

Name:

Date:

LEARN THE WORD	WRITE THEN COVER	WRITE THEN CHECK
hope		
hopeless		
care		
careless		
pain		
painless		
use		
useless		
home		
homeless		
speech		
speechless		
end		
endless		
harm		
harmless		

© Andrew Brodie Publications ✓ PO Box 23, Wellington, Somerset, TA21 8YX ✓ www.andrewbrodie.co.uk

teach	teacher
farm	farmer
drive	driver
mine	miner
babysit	babysitter
run	runner
shop	shopper
spin	spinner

© Andrew Brodie Publications ✓ PO Box 23, Wellington, Somerset, TA21 8YX ✓ www.andrewbrodie.co.uk

Sometimes we have to change the end of a word when we want to add er.

Look carefully at the words on this page.

For these words we <u>just add er:</u>

teach   ⟶ [   ]   farm ⟶ [   ]

For these words we <u>take off e, then add er:</u>

mine   ⟶ [   ]   drive ⟶ [   ]

For these words we <u>double the end consonant, then add er:</u>

babysit ⟶ [   ]   run ⟶ [   ]

shop   ⟶ [   ]   spin ⟶ [   ]

Check that your words look exactly like these:

teacher   farmer   miner   driver   babysitter
    runner   shopper   spinner

Find the correct word to match each clue:

Operates a car   ⟶ [   ]

Milks the cows   ⟶ [   ]

Works at school   ⟶ [   ]

Looks after children when their mum and dad are out   ⟶ [   ]

Runs in race   ⟶ [   ]

Learn, Write, Check.

fold line

1. Look carefully at each word.

2. Say the word out loud.

3. Copy each word in your best handwriting.

4. Look again at the first word, then fold the paper over it to cover it.

5. Write the word in COLUMN 3.

6. Check your spelling.

7. Now do the same for each word.

Name:

Date:

LEARN THE WORD	WRITE THEN COVER	WRITE THEN CHECK
teach		
teacher		
farm		
farmer		
drive		
driver		
mine		
miner		
babysit		
babysitter		
run		
runner		
shop		
shopper		
spin		
spinner		

© Andrew Brodie Publications ✓ PO Box 23, Wellington, Somerset, TA21 8YX ✓ www.andrewbrodie.co.uk

YEAR
3
Term
2

SET
33
Sheet
A

is not	isn't
was not	wasn't
did not	didn't
does not	doesn't
will not	won't
cannot	can't
could not	couldn't
should not	shouldn't

© Andrew Brodie Publications ✓ PO Box 23, Wellington, Somerset, TA21 8YX ✓ www.andrewbrodie.co.uk

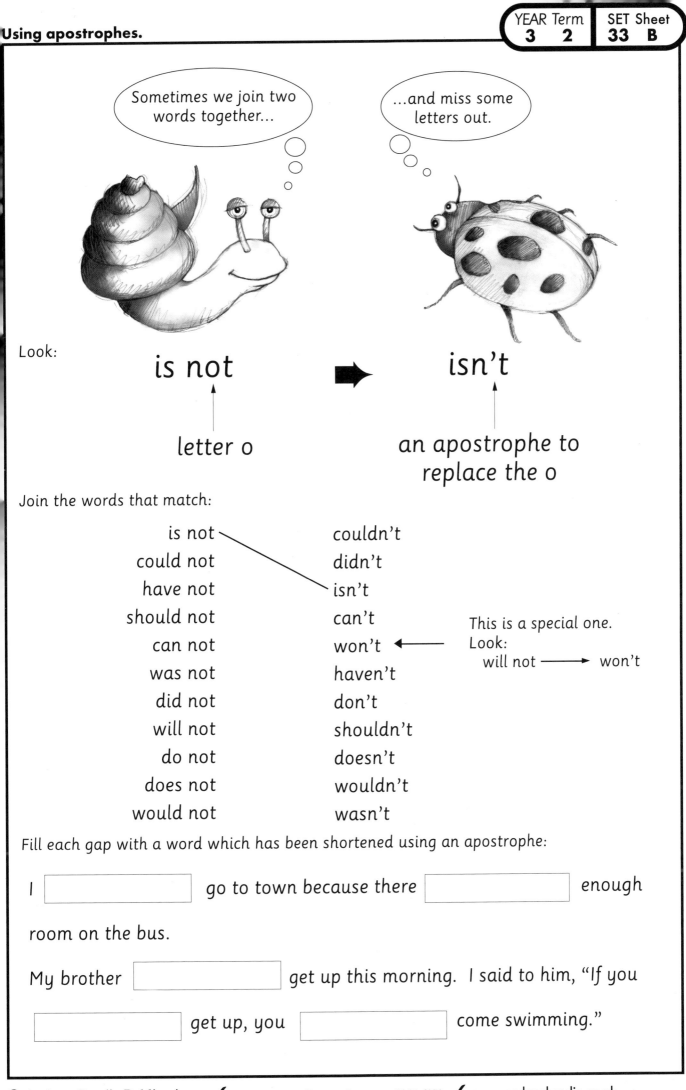

Sometimes we join two words together...

...and miss some letters out.

Look:

is not ➡ isn't

letter o

an apostrophe to replace the o

Join the words that match:

is not	couldn't
could not	didn't
have not	isn't
should not	can't
can not	won't
was not	haven't
did not	don't
will not	shouldn't
do not	doesn't
does not	wouldn't
would not	wasn't

This is a special one. Look:
will not ⟶ won't

Fill each gap with a word which has been shortened using an apostrophe:

I [   ] go to town because there [   ] enough

room on the bus.

My brother [   ] get up this morning. I said to him, "If you

[   ] get up, you [   ] come swimming."

© Andrew Brodie Publications ✓ PO Box 23, Wellington, Somerset, TA21 8YX ✓ www.andrewbrodie.co.uk

fold line

1. Look carefully at each word.

2. Say the word out loud.

3. Copy each word in your best handwriting.

4. Look again at the first word, then fold the paper over it to cover it.

5. Write the word in COLUMN 3.

6. Check your spelling.

7. Now do the same for each word.

Learn, Write, Check.

Name:

Date:

LEARN THE WORD	WRITE THEN COVER	WRITE THEN CHECK
is not		
isn't		
was not		
wasn't		
did not		
didn't		
does not		
doesn't		
will not		
won't		
cannot		
can't		
could not		
couldn't		
should not		
shouldn't		

© Andrew Brodie Publications ✓ PO Box 23, Wellington, Somerset, TA21 8YX ✓ www.andrewbrodie.co.uk

I would	I'd
I have	I've
they have	they've
she will	she'll
there is	there's
where is	where's
here is	here's
they are	they're

© Andrew Brodie Publications ✓ PO Box 23, Wellington, Somerset, TA21 8YX ✓ www.andrewbrodie.co.uk

Where's my shell?

It's on your back.

Look:

where's ➡ where is   it's ➡ it is

Join the words that match in these sets.
We've done some of them for you.

she'll — you will
he'll — she will
you'll — we will
they'll — he will
we'll — I will
I'll — they will

where's — he is
there's — here is
here's — she is
it's — where is
he's — it is
she's — there is

we've — they have
I've — you have
they've — we have
you've — I have

we'd — I would
you'd — we would
I'd — you would

Notice that some words
appear in both of these boxes
but mean different things.

she'd — you had
you'd — I had
I'd — she had

Fill the gaps in this conversation:

" [_____] the dog?" asked Mum.

" [_____] over there," I said.

" [_____] better go and get him," Mum said.

Now write a short conversation of your own.

© Andrew Brodie Publications ✓ PO Box 23, Wellington, Somerset, TA21 8YX ✓ www.andrewbrodie.co.uk

Learn, Write, Check.

fold line

1. Look carefully at each word.

2. Say the word out loud.

3. Copy each word in your best handwriting.

4. Look again at the first word, then fold the paper over it to cover it.

5. Write the word in COLUMN 3.

6. Check your spelling.

7. Now do the same for each word.

Name:

Date:

LEARN THE WORD	WRITE THEN COVER	WRITE THEN CHECK
I would		
I'd		
I have		
I've		
they have		
they've		
she will		
she'll		
there is		
there's		
where is		
where's		
here is		
here's		
they are		
they're		

© Andrew Brodie Publications ✓ PO Box 23, Wellington, Somerset, TA21 8YX ✓ www.andrewbrodie.co.uk

● **Prefixes.**

Sh

behave	misbehave
sense	nonsense
fiction	non-fiction
stop	non-stop
import	export
interior	exterior
star	co-star
clockwise	anticlockwise

© Andrew Brodie Publications ✓ PO Box 23, Wellington, Somerset, TA21 8YX ✓ www.andrewbrodie.co.uk

Prefixes are extra parts added to the start of some words.

They change the meaning of the words.

Practise the word pairs:

behave	misbehave

sense	nonsense

fiction	non-fiction

stop	non-stop

import	export

interior	exterior

star	co-star

clockwise	anticlockwise

Some of the words above give the answers to this crossword.

CLUES DOWN

2.　Not making sense.
7.　Outside a building.
8.　Don't go.

CLUES ACROSS

1.　The direction of a clock's hands.
3.　When you are good, you _____ .
4.　Inside a building.
5.　Story books.
6.　A famous person or something that twinkles in the night sky.

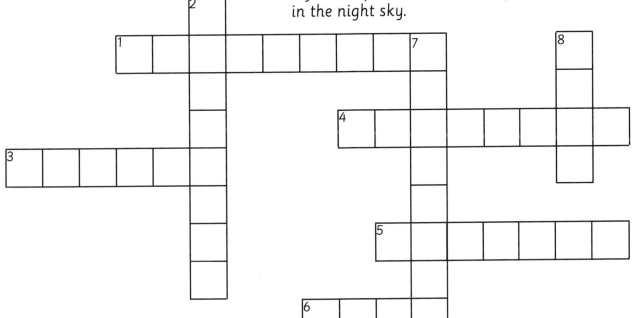

© Andrew Brodie Publications ✓ PO Box 23, Wellington, Somerset, TA21 8YX ✓ www.andrewbrodie.co.uk

Learn, Write, Check.

fold line

1. Look carefully at each word.

2. Say the word out loud.

3. Copy each word in your best handwriting.

4. Look again at the first word, then fold the paper over it to cover it.

5. Write the word in COLUMN 3.

6. Check your spelling.

7. Now do the same for each word.

Name:

Date:

LEARN THE WORD	WRITE THEN COVER	WRITE THEN CHECK
behave		
misbehave		
sense		
nonsense		
fiction		
non-fiction		
stop		
non-stop		
import		
export		
interior		
exterior		
star		
co-star		
clockwise		
anticlockwise		

© Andrew Brodie Publications ✓ PO Box 23, Wellington, Somerset, TA21 8YX ✓ www.andrewbrodie.co.uk

cycle	bicycle
recycle	tricycle
appear	disappear
visible	invisible
normal	abnormal
view	preview
review	interview
marine	submarine

© Andrew Brodie Publications ✓ PO Box 23, Wellington, Somerset, TA21 8YX ✓ www.andrewbrodie.co.uk

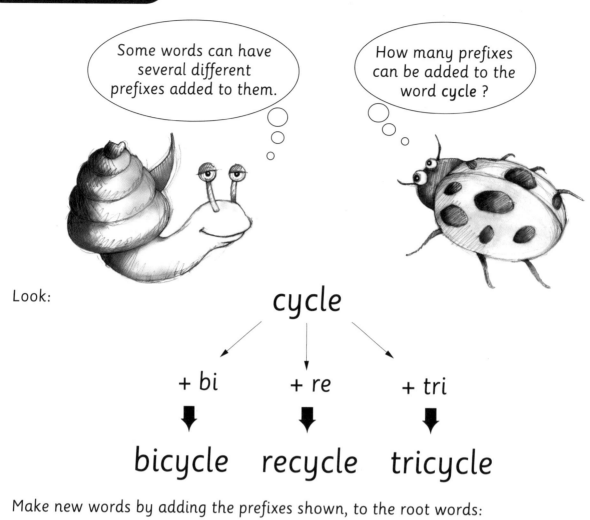

Some words can have several different prefixes added to them.

How many prefixes can be added to the word **cycle** ?

Look:

cycle

+ bi   + re   + tri

bicycle   recycle   tricycle

Make new words by adding the prefixes shown, to the root words:

cycle	+ bi	➡	
cycle	+ re	➡	
cycle	+ tri	➡	
appear	+ dis	➡	
visible	+ in	➡	
normal	+ ab	➡	
view	+ pre	➡	
view	+ re	➡	
view	+ inter	➡	
marine	+ sub	➡	

Can you think of some other words which start with **inter**?

© Andrew Brodie Publications ✓ PO Box 23, Wellington, Somerset, TA21 8YX ✓ www.andrewbrodie.co.uk

Learn, Write, Check.

fold line

1. Look carefully at each word.

2. Say the word out loud.

3. Copy each word in your best handwriting.

4. Look again at the first word, then fold the paper over it to cover it.

5. Write the word in COLUMN 3.

6. Check your spelling.

7. Now do the same for each word.

Name:

Date:

LEARN THE WORD	WRITE THEN COVER	WRITE THEN CHECK
cycle		
bicycle		
recycle		
tricycle		
appear		
disappear		
visible		
invisible		
normal		
abnormal		
view		
preview		
review		
interview		
marine		
submarine		

© Andrew Brodie Publications ✓ PO Box 23, Wellington, Somerset, TA21 8YX ✓ www.andrewbrodie.co.uk

YEAR 3
Term 3
SET 37
Sheet A

Monday	Tuesday
Wednesday	Thursday
Friday	Saturday
Sunday	holiday
yesterday	tomorrow
birthday	anniversary
weekday	weekend
fortnight	tonight

© Andrew Brodie Publications ✓ PO Box 23, Wellington, Somerset, TA21 8YX ✓ www.andrewbrodie.co.uk

Write the days of the week in the right order.

Try to make no mistakes with the spellings.

JUMBLED DAYS

Wednesday   Saturday   Monday   Friday
Sunday   Thursday   Tuesday

1 _____

2 _____

3 _____

4 _____

5 _____

6 _____

7 _____

Here are some more words to do with days:

holiday   yesterday   tomorrow   birthday   anniversary   week
weekday   weekend   fortnight   tonight   today

Solve this puzzle using some of the words.

CLUES ACROSS

2. I like the summer _____ .
3. The day after today.
4. I might have a party for my _____ .
6. The two days which are not school days.
7. This day itself.

CLUES DOWN

1. Two weeks make a _____ .
5. The day before today.
7. I will go to bed _____.

1. Look carefully at each word.

2. Say the word out loud.

3. Copy each word in your best handwriting.

4. Look again at the first word, then fold the paper over it to cover it.

5. Write the word in COLUMN 3.

6. Check your spelling.

7. Now do the same for each word.

Learn, Write, Check.

Name:

Date:

LEARN THE WORD	WRITE THEN COVER	WRITE THEN CHECK
Monday		
Tuesday		
Wednesday		
Thursday		
Friday		
Saturday		
Sunday		
holiday		
yesterday		
tomorrow		
birthday		
anniversary		
weekday		
weekend		
fortnight		
tonight		

© Andrew Brodie Publications ✓ PO Box 23, Wellington, Somerset, TA21 8YX ✓ www.andrewbrodie.co.uk

YEAR
3
Term
3
SET
38
Sheet
A

January

February

March

April

May

June

July

August

September

October

November

December

spring

summer

autumn

fwinter

© Andrew Brodie Publications ✓ PO Box 23, Wellington, Somerset, TA21 8YX ✓ www.andrewbrodie.co.uk

Some months have thirty days and some have thirty-one days.

February is strange. It has twenty-eight days and twenty-nine days in a leap year.

Copy out this rhyme in your best handwriting.

> Thirty days has September,
> April, June and November.
> All the rest have thirty-one,
>   except for February alone,
> Which has twenty-eight days clear
> and twenty-nine in each leap year.

_____

_____

_____

_____

_____

_____

_____

_____

Which month usually has 28 days? [   ]

Which months have 30 days?

[   ] [   ] [   ] [   ]

Which months have 31 days?

[   ] [   ] [   ] [   ]

[   ] [   ] [   ]

© Andrew Brodie Publications ✓ PO Box 23, Wellington, Somerset, TA21 8YX ✓ www.andrewbrodie.co.uk

fold line

3. Copy each word in your best handwriting.

4. Look again at the first word, then fold the paper over it to cover it.

Learn, Write, Check.

YEAR 3 Term 3
SET 38 Sheet C

1. Look carefully at each word.

2. Say the word out loud.

5. Write the word in COLUMN 3.

6. Check your spelling.

7. Now do the same for each word.

Name:

Date:

LEARN THE WORD	WRITE THEN COVER	WRITE THEN CHECK
January		
February		
March		
April		
May		
June		
July		
August		
September		
October		
November		
December		
spring		
summer		
autumn		
winter		

© Andrew Brodie Publications ✓ PO Box 23, Wellington, Somerset, TA21 8YX ✓ www.andrewbrodie.co.uk

YEAR
3
Term
3

SET
39
Sheet
A

eleven	twelve
thirteen	fourteen
fifteen	sixteen
seventeen	eighteen
nineteen	twenty
thirty	forty
fifty	sixty
seventy	eighty

© Andrew Brodie Publications ✓ PO Box 23, Wellington, Somerset, TA21 8YX ✓ www.andrewbrodie.co.uk

We sometimes write numbers using numerals...

...and sometimes we use words.

NUMBER WORD BANK

eleven   twelve   thirteen   fourteen   fifteen

sixteen   seventeen   eighteen   nineteen   twenty

thirty   forty   fifty   sixty   seventy   eighty

Write the correct words to match the numbers written in numerals.

NUMERALS	WORDS	NUMERALS	WORDS
20	twenty	13	
17		80	
11		12	
60		70	
16		14	
19		40	
50		18	
30		15	

Look, these words have a letter u: four   fourteen

This word does not have a letter u: forty

© Andrew Brodie Publications ✔ PO Box 23, Wellington, Somerset, TA21 8YX ✔ www.andrewbrodie.co.uk

Learn, Write, Check.

1. Look carefully at each word.

2. Say the word out loud.

fold line

3. Copy each word in your best handwriting.

4. Look again at the first word, then fold the paper over it to cover it.

5. Write the word in COLUMN 3.

6. Check your spelling.

7. Now do the same for each word.

Name:

Date:

LEARN THE WORD	WRITE THEN COVER	WRITE THEN CHECK
eleven		
twelve		
thirteen		
fourteen		
fifteen		
sixteen		
seventeen		
eighteen		
nineteen		
twenty		
thirty		
forty		
fifty		
sixty		
seventy		
eighty		

© Andrew Brodie Publications ✓ PO Box 23, Wellington, Somerset, TA21 8YX ✓ www.andrewbrodie.co.uk

ninety	hundred
thousand	million
metre	centimetre
millimetre	kilometre
gram	kilogram
litre	millilitre
second	minute
hour	month

© Andrew Brodie Publications ✓ PO Box 23, Wellington, Somerset, TA21 8YX ✓ www.andrewbrodie.co.uk

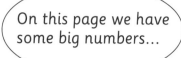

On this page we have some big numbers...

...and some words to do with measuring.

Match the numerals to the number words.

90 — thousand

100 — ninety

1000 — million

1000000 — hundred

Copy the words.

Label the hands on the clock, using these words: second   minute   hour

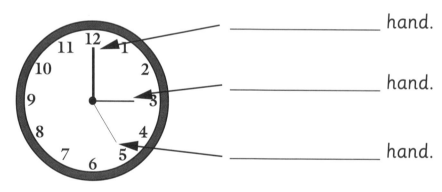

_____ hand.

_____ hand.

_____ hand.

Write the correct measurement word for each abbreviation:

MEASUREMENT WORDS

metre   centimetre   millimetre   kilometre
    gram   kilogram   litre   millilitre

cm ⟶ [   ]   km ⟶ [   ]

m ⟶ [   ]   l ⟶ [   ]

ml ⟶ [   ]   kg ⟶ [   ]

mm ⟶ [   ]   g ⟶ [   ]

© Andrew Brodie Publications ✓ PO Box 23, Wellington, Somerset, TA21 8YX ✓ www.andrewbrodie.co.uk

Learn, Write, Check.

fold line

3. Copy each word in your best handwriting.

4. Look again at the first word, then fold the paper over it to cover it.

1. Look carefully at each word.

2. Say the word out loud.

5. Write the word in COLUMN 3.

6. Check your spelling.

7. Now do the same for each word.

Name:

Date:

LEARN THE WORD	WRITE THEN COVER	WRITE THEN CHECK
ninety		
hundred		
thousand		
million		
metre		
centimetre		
millimetre		
kilometre		
gram		
kilogram		
litre		
millilitre		
second		
minute		
hour		
month		

© Andrew Brodie Publications ✓ PO Box 23, Wellington, Somerset, TA21 8YX ✓ www.andrewbrodie.co.uk

Some of the activities on Sheet B for each set of words require answ
which are individual to the pupils. Some, however, have standard a
and we list these below to save time for teachers in marking pupils'

Set 1, Sheet B ringing, walking, jumping, painting, dressing, resting, calling
Missing words: dressing, jumping, calling, painting, ringing, singing

Set 2, Sheet B dreaming, feeling, shouting, sailing, boiling, peeling, speaking
Missing words: sweeping, sailing, nailing, eating, treating, looking, cooking

Set 3, Sheet B hopping, sitting, skipping, stepping, gripping, shutting, winning
Missing words: skipping, skipping, gripping, shutting, running
humming, winning, spinning, swimming, stopping

Set 4, Sheet B coming, smiling, taking, caring, making, dividing, staring
Root words: shine, tune, rhyme, time

Set 5, Sheet B double z: dazzle, nuzzle, puzzle   double b: wobble, dribble, nibble
double d: middle, muddle, saddle, fiddle, puddle, paddle
double g: giggle, wiggle   double t: little, nettle, kettle, rattle, cattle

Set 6, Sheet B trickling, pickling, prickling, crackling, tackling, chuckling, buckling
Missing words: pickle, trickling, chuckling

Set 7, Sheet B able words: able, table, valuable, cable, vegetable, portable, reliable, probabl
ible words: horrible, sensible, terrible, possible, invisible, impossible, visible, respon
Extension activity: lovable, forgivable, believable, movable, removable

Set 8, Sheet B Cannot end in ing: thimble, fable, simple, example
Letter u followed by letter m: crumple, bumble, jumble, mumble, tumble,
grumble, stumble
Letter o followed by letter u: double, trouble
Letter m but no letter u: thimble, scramble, simple, example, sample
Words ending in ple: crumple, simple, example, sample

Set 9, Sheet B ...cle words: miracle, cycle, uncle, circle, bicycle, icicle
...dle words: candle, trundle, handle, bundle, needle
...gle words: bungle, jungle, single, jingle, tingle

Set 10, Sheet B untidy, unlucky, unusual, unzip, untie, unfair, unkind
Missing words: unhappy, unzip, untie, unkind (or unfair)

Set 11, Sheet B disagree, disappear, disconnect, dishonest, disobey

Set 12, Sheet B revisit, replay, rewrite, recycle, replace, return

Set 13, Sheet B faster, fastest   slower, slowest   quicker, quickest   colder, coldest

© Andrew Brodie Publications ✓ PO Box 23, Wellington, Somerset, TA21 8YX ✓ www.andrewbrodie.co.uk

ANSWERS

14, Sheet B closer, closest wider, widest safer, safest nicer, nicest

						6 w									
						i		7 l				8 n			
						d		a			4 w	i	d	e	r
		2 c	5 l	o	s	e	s	t				c			
			a			s		e				e			
			t			t		3 s	a	f	e	s	t		
1 n	i	c	e	r				t				t			
			r												

t 15, Sheet B bigger, biggest fitter, fittest sadder, saddest
t 16, Sheet B foggier, foggiest wavier, waviest funnier, funniest luckier, luckiest
t 17, Sheet B inky, fully, fussy, moody, dreamy, cheeky
t 18, Sheet B funny, runny, tinny, poppy, dotty, ratty, batty
Missing words: ratty, poppy, fun, funny
t 19, Sheet B lazy, easy, shiny, rosy, stony, breezy, bony
Missing words: smoky, laze, easy, shiny
t 20, Sheet B tables, desks, windows, books, times, houses
t 21, Sheet B catches, pushes, blushes, boxes, matches, brushes, foxes, churches
watch: watches ditch: ditches fax: faxes fizz: fizzes
t 22, Sheet B keys, trays, monkeys, plays, holidays, birthdays, buys
t 23, Sheet B ladies, puppies, ponies, parties, pennies, hobbies, flies
Missing words: puppies, parties, flies, pennies
t 24, Sheet B men, women, children teeth, geese, feet mice, headlice
calves, halves, wolves, shelves
t 25, Sheet B silent **h**: rhyme, honest, where, when silent **w**: wrap, wrapping, write, wrist
silent **g**: gnome, gnat silent **k**: knives, kneel, knee, knock, knife, know
t 26, Sheet B silent **b**: crumb, bomb, comb, thumb, lamb, numb
silent **l**: halves, could, palm, should, half, calm, calf, calves, would
t 27, Sheet B bedroom, thing, somewhere, body, something, everyone, playground
one, sometimes, motorway
t 28, Sheet B Pupils can choose any eight compound words from those listed here:
pan, cake: pancake down, stairs: downstairs up, stairs: upstairs
(up, end: up-end) any, one: anyone any, thing: anything
any, body: anybody any, where: anywhere goal, keeper: goalkeeper
week, end: weekend break, fast: breakfast some, one: someone
some, thing: something some, body: somebody some, where: somewhere
some, times: sometimes
t 29, Sheet B lovely, likely, really, regularly, nicely, safely, usually, properly
Missing words: likely, really, safely
t 30, Sheet B hopeful, useful, cheerful, painful, wonderful, careful
t 31, Sheet B hopeless, painless, homeless, endless, careless, useless, speechless, harmless
Missing words: harmless, painless, careless
Crossword: Across: 1. speechless 3. hopeless 4. endless 5. painless
Down: 2. careless 3. harmless
t 32, Sheet B teacher, farmer
miner, driver
babysitter, shopper, runner, spinner
Missing words: driver, farmer, teacher, babysitter, runner

ANSWERS

Set 33, Sheet B

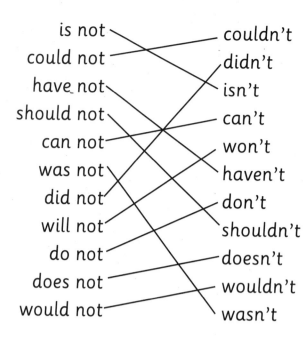

is not — isn't
could not — couldn't
have not — haven't
should not — shouldn't
can not — can't
was not — wasn't
did not — didn't
will not — won't
do not — don't
does not — doesn't
would not — wouldn't

Missing words:
couldn't, wasn't
wouldn't, don't
can't

Set 34, Sheet B

she'll — she will
he'll — he will
you'll — you will
they'll — they will
we'll — we will
I'll — I will

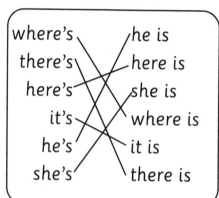

where's — where is
there's — there is
here's — here is
it's — it is
he's — he is
she's — she is

we've — we have
I've — I have
they've — they have
you've — you have

we'd — we would
you'd — you would
I'd — I would

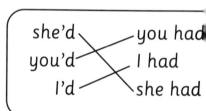

she'd — she had
you'd — you had
I'd — I had

Missing words: Where's, He's, You'd

Set 35, Sheet B Answers across: 1. clockwise 3. behave 4. interior 5. fiction 6. star
Answers down: 2. nonsense 7. exterior 8. stop

Set 36, Sheet B bicycle, recycle, tricycle, disappear, invisible, abnormal, preview, review interview, submarine

Set 37, Sheet B 1. Monday 2. Tuesday 3. Wednesday 4. Thursday 5. Friday
6. Saturday 7. Sunday
Answers across: 2. holiday 3. tomorrow 4. birthday 6. weekend 7. today
Answers down: 1. fortnight 5. yesterday 7. tonight

Set 38, Sheet B February   April, June, September, November
January, March, May, July, August, October, December

Set 39, Sheet B 1st column: seventeen, eleven, sixty, sixteen, nineteen, fifty, thirty
2nd column: thirteen, eighty, twelve, seventy, fourteen, forty, eighteen, fift

Set 40, Sheet B Clock hands: minute, hour, second

© Andrew Brodie Publications ✓ PO Box 23, Wellington, Somerset, TA21 8YX ✓ www.andrewbrodie.co.uk